Our Pacific Northwest

Birds & Habitat

Featuring the Puget Sound Area

Written by Joy Johnson
Photographs & layout by Craig Johnson
Research by Joy & Craig Johnson

Printed in the Pacific Northwest, USA
by Printing Control, using
Forest Stewardship Council approved paper.

ORANGE SPOT PUBLISHING

Preface

I have never before published most of these photos, but did include some in this volume from our previous books that best represent the species shown. With many new images, this is an excellent companion to those books. And because this is the most comprehensive book Joy and I have ever published, it also stands nicely on its own.

We are both Pacific Northwest natives who love this area's natural beauty. As an illustrator, watercolor painter and graphic designer for more than three decades, I took photographs mainly to gain research for my paintings, which ranged from ships to animal portraits. In 2004, my love for birds drew me to photograph them in the field. My passion increased each year, as did my collection of bird images. Joy and I would use any excuse to go out to find and photograph birds. I took photos while hiking, camera in hand, as Joy helped spot birds with her binoculars. All my photos were hand-held using SLR digital cameras (ranging from 6-12 megapixels) and a 400 mm, f/5.6 lens, often with a 1.4x teleconverter. This freedom of movement allowed me to meet the birds "eye to eye." A successful photo was one where I captured the image without startling the bird and left it in the same location as when I first noticed it. No photo is worth jeopardizing a bird's well being.

I've used my bird photographs primarily to help others see and understand these marvelous creatures. Joy and I study ornithology and enjoy conveying this information through our books, presentations, website, and also by donating photos to wildlife preservation organizations.

- Craig

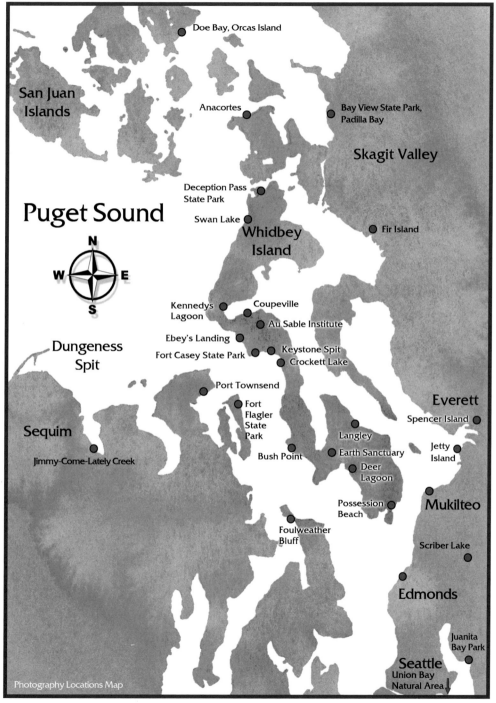

Doe Bay, Orcas Island

San Juan
Islands

Anacortes

Bay View State Park,
Padilla Bay

Skagit Valley

Deception Pass
State Park

Puget Sound

Swan Lake

Whidbey
Island

Fir Island

N
W   E
S

Kennedys
Lagoon

Coupeville

Au Sable Institute

Dungeness
Spit

Ebey's Landing

Fort Casey State Park

Keystone Spit

Crockett Lake

Port Townsend

Everett

Sequim

Fort
Flagler
State
Park

Spencer Island

Langley

Jetty
Island

Jimmy-Come-Lately Creek

Bush Point

Earth Sanctuary

Deer
Lagoon

Mukilteo

Possession
Beach

Foulweather
Bluff

Scriber Lake

Edmonds

Juanita
Bay Park

Seattle
Union Bay
Natural Area

Photography Locations Map

Cape Flattery

Washington State

Olympic
National Forest

Hurricane
Ridge

Ocean
Shores

Potholes

Othello

Nisqually National
Wildlife Refuge

Umtanum Creek

Tokeland

Wenas Basin

Fort Simcoe State Park

Ridgefield National
Wildlife Refuge

Vancouver

Table of Contents

Woodland - Riparian — 4

Dry Interior — 42

Wetland - Agricultural — 43

Beach - Offshore — 74

Foothills - Mountain — 92

Index - References — 96

Watercolor paintings
by Craig Johnson

Woodland ~ Riparian

Woodland and riparian, or river's edge, habitats support a wide variety of birds. Protective cover, food, and fresh water found in these areas are essential to the survival of many resident and migratory species. In the Puget Sound region, with its numerous rivers and wooded areas, birds often use both types of habitat at different times of the year.

Cassin's Finch, female   Wenas Basin

Warbling Vireo   Fort Casey State Park

Stumbling upon a small flock of foraging warblers is a magical experience. Bright flashes of yellow, spied through shadowed leaves, keep us apprised of their ever-moving presence.

Orange-crowned Warbler   Fort Flagler State Park

Common Yellowthroat, male

Wilson's Warbler, male

Townsend's Warbler, male   Fort Casey State Park

Yellow-rumped Warbler "Myrtle", female

Since warblers tend to flock together, finding one type of warbler can lead to another. Parasitic Brown-headed Cowbirds also may be seen in the same vicinity during breeding season, as female cowbirds may lay an egg in a warbler nest, leaving the unsuspecting warbler parents to raise their young.

Brown-headed Cowbird, male   Fort Casey State Park

6

Yellow-rumped Warbler "Audubon's", male
Earth Sanctuary

Cedar Waxwing   Earth Sanctuary

Cedar Waxwings are known for their affinity to fruit, but they also flycatch. In early summer we witnessed a large flock sallying insects over a pond, as well as gleaning them from surrounding lily pads.

Cedar Waxwing, juvenile

Cedar Waxwing,
Whidbey Island

Bullock's Oriole, juvenile

Dazzling migrants, such as the Western Tanager and Bullock's Oriole, will bring a smile of appreciation to even a casual observer. Their tropical appearance is a refreshing reminder of summer. Both of these species will often be in the upper canopy, blending with the shadows in spite of the males' bright plumage.

Western Tanager, female

Bullock's Oriole, male Possession Beach

Western Tanager, male

Western Tanager, male
Umtanum Creek

Black-headed Grosbeak, male   Orcas Island

Migratory Black-headed Grosbeaks are fairly common here from May to August. Evening Grosbeaks can be seen year-round, though they typically move to higher elevations to breed.

Black-headed Grosbeak, female

Evening Grosbeak, female   Wenas Basin

Evening Grosbeak, male
Wenas Basin

Not much bigger than a hummingbird, the Golden-crowned Kinglet is North America's smallest songbird. Photographing tiny birds has the added reward of being able to enlarge the image to see details not easily viewable while in the field, such as the bright orange, reptile-like scales covering this bird's feet.

Golden-crowned Kinglet

Golden-crowned Kinglet
Fort Casey State Park

Black-capped Chickadee

Ruby-crowned Kinglet   Possession Beach

Always hand holding his camera, Craig was able to capture images spontaneously, like this Ruby-crowned Kinglet that just caught a fly. In this photo, the depth of field made the background appear to be a solid color, even though it was actually a jumble of branches.

Ruby-crowned Kinglet, male   Possession Beach

Anna's Hummingbird, female

Anna's female feeding fledgling

Anna's Hummingbird, male

Increasingly found in the Puget Sound region year-round, Anna's Hummingbirds have successfully expanded their range from California by foraging on cultivated winter-blooming plants and hummingbird feeders in populated areas.

The first record of Anna's hummers nesting in Washington State was in the mid 1970s.

Anna's Hummingbird, male
Whidbey Island

Anna's Hummingbird, male

Rufous Hummingbird, female, collecting nesting material from a cattail

Rufous Hummingbirds make the longest migration of any bird per their size. They require woodland area near a water source, such as a pond, to successfully breed.

To view a full Rufous Hummingbird nesting experience, eggs to fledglings, visit our website, www.pugetsoundbackyardbirds.com

Rufous Hummingbird, male

Rufous nest and eggs

Rufous hatchlings, first day

Rufous Hummingbird nestlings   Earth Sanctuary

Flocking together in the winter, Bushtits are sometimes seen in groups of up to 60 birds. Gleaning insects and seeds off shrubs and trees, they quickly move on to the next location.

Bushtit, male

Bushtit, female
Bush Point

Bushtit, male

14

In the springtime, wrens may perch more conspicuously on a high point of a shrub or bramble to sing their exuberant songs. Of the four species of wren found in the Puget Sound area, the House Wren is the only one that is entirely migratory.

House Wren

Pacific (Winter) Wren

Bewick's Wren   Possession Beach   15

With icicles formed on nearby branches, this Spotted Towhee was hunkered down, absorbing some sun on a cold winter afternoon after doing his two-footed foraging dance in the leaf litter below.

Spotted Towhee, juvenile

Members of the sparrow family, Dark-eyed Juncos are also ground feeders, searching mainly for seeds, plus insects and spiders.

Plump larvae make a high protein meal for an eager fledgling.

Dark-eyed Junco, adult with larvae

Dark-eyed Junco, juvenile

Dark-eyed Junco, adult & juvenile

Dark-eyed Junco, male   Bush Point

Both the striking Red Crossbills and Pine Siskins are nomadic species, flying to areas with the best available food sources.

Red Crossbills can breed any time they locate a large enough cone crop, the mainstay of their diet, even in winter. Using their uniquely shaped bill, they readily remove conifer seeds to eat and feed their young.

Red Crossbill, female   Bush Point

Pine Siskin

Red Crossbill, male
Orcas Island

Red Crossbills
Fort Casey State Park

Acrobatic chickadees dangle expertly to extract cone seeds, which are part of their diet in the winter. During the breeding season, they primarily take caterpillars to feed their nestlings.

Chestnut-backed Chickadee, juvenile waiting to be fed by parent

Chestnut-backed Chickadee Fort Casey State Park

Chestnut-backed Chickadee   Fort Casey State Park

A visitor to the lowlands during colder months of the year, the Varied Thrush often mixes with flocks of American Robins. In late fall we regularly see them feasting on the apples remaining on our trees.

Varied Thrush, female   Langley

Varied Thrush, male   Bush Point

Varied Thrush, male   Earth Sanctuary

With their squat body shape, thin legs, and pointy bills, different types of thrushes do have similarities. However, the Hermit Thrush, true to its name, is much more difficult to spot than the American Robin. It might best be seen on the edge of a woodland habitat, when it pops out briefly to search the ground for insects.

American Robin, juvenile

American Robin, female

American Robin, male

When looking for flycatchers, like the Pacific-slope, Western Wood-Pewee, and Eastern Kingbird, it helps to first listen for their songs. When singing, they are likely on a perch and more visible.

The generally inconspicuous Lincoln's Sparrow likes brushy areas near a river, stream or marsh.

Western Wood-Pewee   Possession Beach

Lincoln's Sparrow   Spencer Island

Eastern Kingbird   Spencer Island

Pacific-slope Flycatcher
Fort Casey State Park

Watching a Swainson's Thrush collect a bill full of insects to feed fledglings hidden in the shrubs was a summertime treat. We were alerted to their presence when the young begged loudly as the adult approached.

Cryptically colored for concealment against the bark, Brown Creepers may only be noticed when ascending a tree trunk in their characteristic spiral manner.

Swainson's Thrush, juvenile

Brown Creeper   Earth Sanctuary

White-crowned Sparrow adult feeding juvenile

Found in a variety of habitats, sparrows typically forage on the ground or low foliage. Bills showing juicy red evidence, the Golden-crowned Sparrow, pictured here, and Fox Sparrow (opposite) were busy eating remnants of the previous year's blackberry crop, a favored winter food.

White-crowned Sparrow
Possession Beach

Golden-crowned Sparrow   Whidbey Island

Song Sparrow

House Sparrow, female

Fox Sparrow   Bush Point

Both avid seed eaters, House Finches are more commonly seen than Purple Finches. Color variations in the red feathering of House Finches occur based on the amount of pigment in foods consumed during a molt. Males may range from yellowish to dark red, with darker red birds being preferred by female House Finches.

Purple Finch, male

Purple Finch, female

House Finch, male & female   Port Townsend

American Goldfinches can really liven up a gray northwest spring day. Welcome feeder birds, they can also be seen in a number of habitat areas, having a preference for those near open expanses of weeds. Similar looking Lesser Goldfinch may be seen in a small portion of Klickitat County, south-central Washington.

American Goldfinch, male

Lesser Goldfinch, male

American Goldfinch, female, with nesting material

American Goldfinch, juvenile   Orcas Island

Red-breasted Sapsuckers and Lewis's Woodpeckers both are known to catch flying insects on the wing. Sapsuckers also drill small sap wells to feed on the sap that drips out with their bristle-tipped tongues. These sap wells are a food source for many other species of birds, as well as insects and some mammals.

Lewis's Woodpecker   Fort Simcoe State Park

Earth Sanctuary

Red-breasted
Sapsucker

Red-breasted Sapsucker   Earth Sanctuary

Strong legs and zygodactyl feet, meaning two toes forward and two toes backward, are ideal for the vertical lifestyle of a woodpecker. Clinging to tree trunks, woodpeckers then use their stiff tail feathers as a brace. Wood-boring beetles and their larvae and other insects make up the majority of a woodpecker's diet. When feeding young, the Downy will add tent caterpillars to the menu.

Downy Woodpecker male

Downy Woodpecker, male

Hairy Woodpecker, female

Hairy Woodpecker male

Hairy Woodpecker, juvenile male

29

Ants make up the majority of the Northern Flicker's diet. Woodland edges that have open area nearby are preferred habitat, where they can readily probe for subterranean ant tunnels with their long, pointed bills and highly extendible tongues.

Newly on her own, the young bird below was working hard to dig insects out of the grass, but from what we could see, she was coming up with more dirt than anything else!

Northern Flicker, adult male feeding juvenile male

Northern Flicker, male

Northern Flicker, female

Northern Flicker, juvenile female   Fort Casey State Park

A pair of Pileated Woodpeckers will create a new nest cavity each year, plus multiple roosting holes. The following year, other birds or mammals that cannot create their own cavity nests will make use of abandoned ones.

Using their stout, pointed bills, Pileated Woodpeckers drum to communicate with other wood-peckers and hammer or chisel to create a hole. An adult may strike a hard surface with its bill up to twenty times per second. Strong neck and jaw muscles work together to achieve this feat while spongy cartilage between the bill and reinforced skull helps absorb the impact of each strike.

Pileated Woodpecker, female at nest cavity

Pileated Woodpecker, juvenile female and adult female

Pileated Woodpecker, juvenile female

Pileated Woodpecker, male   Spencer Island

Members of the Corvid Family, crafty jays and magpies are related to crows. Known for their wide variety of vocalizations, Steller's Jays may even mimic other species, including two that we hear regularly, Red-tailed Hawks and cats.

The Balck-billed magpie is a species found east of the Cascades.

Western Scrub-Jay   Vancouver

Black-billed Magpie   Yakima

Red-breasted Nuthatch, male   Bush Point

Feisty Red-breasted Nuthatches are only four inches long, but make up for their small size with attitude, giving chase to larger hole-nesting birds without hesitation. Their practice of placing resin from coniferous trees around the entrance of their nest holes may serve to keep out predators or competitors. To avoid the sticky substance, the nuthatch will dive directly through the hole, without touching the sides.

Red-breasted Nuthatch, juvenile   Doe Bay

Red-breasted Nuthatch, male

Red-breasted Nuthatch, female

Rock Pigeons and Mourning Doves use a variety of habitats and have adapted to living around human development. Band-tailed Pigeons breed in more forested or dense riparian areas.

Rock Pigeon

Band-tailed Pigeon

Mourning Doves, female and male

34   Mourning Dove, female   Coupeville

Members of the accipiter family, Cooper's and Sharp-shinned Hawks are experts at navigating through a tangle of branches and foliage, deftly pursuing smaller birds at high speeds.

Cooper's Hawk, with American Robin

Cooper's Hawk, juvenile

Sharp-shinned Hawk, juvenile

Cooper's Hawk
Whidbey Island

35

Great Horned Owl

Great Horned Owl, fledgling

Skillful predators with exceptional hearing and keen low-light vision, owls' velvety soft wings help them to silently hunt their quarry under cover of darkness. Glimpsing these beautiful creatures in the daytime is always a pleasant surprise.

Barred Owl   South Whidbey State Park

Barn Owl   Whidbey Island

Adept at sallying flying insects from a perch, flycatchers are attracted to riparian habitats or woodland edges with water nearby.

Although not in the flycatcher family, the Townsend's Solitaire is also quite able to catch aerial insects or it may drop quickly to the ground to nab a spider.

The White-breasted Nuthatch prefers to glean insects from tree trunks.

Ash-throated Flycatcher   Fort Simcoe S.P.

Olive-sided Flycatcher
Possession Beach

White-breasted
Nuthatch

Willow Flycatcher
Possession Beach

Townsend's Solitaire   Fort Flagler State Park

Sage Thrasher

Swainson's Thrush

Chipping Sparrow   Wenas Basin

Typically found in eastern Washington, Say's Phoebes, like many other migratory birds, will use different types of habitat on their flights to and from breeding grounds.

All of these birds might be found in the Wenas Basin area of eastern Washington during the summer.

Say's Phoebe   Wenas Basin

Common Raven   Orcas Island

Common Raven Pair

Highly intelligent, ravens are clever problem solvers and, as omnivores, use a variety of methods to acquire their food.

This Common Raven came quite close to Craig, seemingly curious about what he was doing.

Very social creatures, American Crows form monogamous pairs and perform bonding behaviors, such as allo-preening shown here. Offspring from a previous breeding season may stay with their parents to cooperatively help raise the next year's young, presumably learning skills to improve their future nesting success.

American Crow, juvenile

American Crow pair   Keystone Spit

Dry Interior

Dry interior habitat occurs in areas east of the Cascade Mountains with open, arid conditions. Places like the Potholes may host the birds shown here at certain times of the year. Some open grassy areas west of the Cascades are favorable for Savannah Sparrows all year and during winter for Northern Shrikes.

Northern Shrike
Crockett Lake,
Whidbey Island

Loggerhead Shrike
Potholes Wildlife Area

Savannah Sparrow
Keystone Spit, Whidbey Island

Lark Sparrow   Eastern WA

Wetland - Agricultural

Areas where the surface soil is saturated or covered with water are considered wetlands. Estuarine wetlands form where freshwater and saltwater meet and mix. These swamp and marsh areas are generally rich in plant life and insects, and thus support an array of birds and animals. Land cultivated for agricultural use creates another type of open habitat, often with wetland intermixed, forming various micro-habitats.

Spencer Island, Everett

Marsh Wren

Marsh Wren   Deer Lagoon, Whidey Island

Northern Harrier, male

Having facial disks similar to owls, Northern Harriers rely on hearing as well as vision when flying low over fields searching for prey.

Northern Harrier, male

Northern Harrier, female

Northern Harrier, female   Crockett Lake

With moth-like wing movements, Short-eared Owls can regularly be seen hunting at Whidbey Island's Crockett Lake and Keystone Spit during the winter months. Snowy Owls are irregular visitors in this region, showing up when the winter food supply further north is insufficient.

Short-eared Owl

Snowy Owl   Keystone Spit

Short-eared Owl

Short-eared Owl   Crockett Lake

Short-eared Owl   Keystone Spit

Large Red-tailed Hawks may stand out when perched on a post or high tree branch overlooking an open expanse of field.

There are 16 subspecies of this impressive buteo, determined by variations in size, color and tail markings, which can make Red-tailed Hawks confusing to accurately identify.

Red-tailed Hawk, juvenile

Red-tailed Hawk

Red-tailed Hawk

Hunting primarily from an elevated perch, Red-tailed Hawks will take small mammals, medium sized birds, reptiles and amphibians. The hawk below had just captured a bird near Whidbey Island's Crockett Lake and proceeded to remove the feathers.

Red-tailed Hawk, juvenile   Ebey's Landing

Red-tailed Hawk

Red-tailed Hawk

Rough-legged Hawk
Skagit Valley

Ruffled feather "pantaloons" help keep Rough-legged Hawks warm on their arctic and sub-arctic breeding grounds. They venture south to spend the winter in the lower 48 states, including the Skagit flats and parts of eastern Washington.

Rough-legged Hawk, juvenile   Ridgefield NWR

Turkey Vulture   Orcas Island

Swainson's Hawk   Wenas Basin

Birds of prey make good use of man-made structures throughout and beside farm fields. These prominent perches make excellent vantage points from which to scan for a potential meal.

Primarily using their keen olfactory sense, Turkey Vultures find carrion in pastures and along roadsides.

Gyrfalcon   Skagit Valley

Peregrine Falcon   Skagit Valley

Merlin, female   Ebey's Landing

Our smallest falcon, the American Kestrel, might be seen at Greenbank Farm on Whidbey Island. It may wind-hover in an open meadow before diving down dramatically to capture its prey, which mainly consists of large insects, like grasshoppers, but also small rodents, birds, reptiles and amphibians.

American Kestrel, female   Coupeville

American Kestrel, male
Greenbank Farm

Peregrine
Falcon,
juvenile

Bald Eagle   Crockett Lake

In stark contrast, the Bald Eagle is a more formidable predator, taking large birds, small mammals, such as rabbits, and carrion, in addition to their mainstay of fish.

Bald Eagle, juvenile

Bald Eagle,
atop a utility pole,
Crockett Lake

Masters at hawking flying insects, swallows capture copious amounts of them when feeding their young, making them welcome neighbors.

Some swallows will incorporate feathers from other birds into their nests. These downy linings help keep nestlings warm, allowing them to grow faster.

Cliff Swallow   Spencer Island

Violet-green Swallow, male   Skagit Valley

Tree Swallow
Ebey's Landing

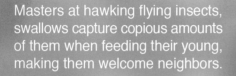

Northern Rough-winged Swallow

Purple Martin, male

Swallows tend to do well around humans and have adapted to using nest boxes, or gourds in the case of Purple Martins, though natural habitat is better for the birds' overall longevity.

Barn Swallow, juvenile   Possession Beach wetland area

Agricultural fields offer suitable conditions for a variety of species at different times of the year. Those adjacent to undeveloped wetlands are especially important to humans, as they are buffer zones that collect excess precipitation to abate potential flooding, and to wildlife, providing rich habitat for birds and other creatures.

Game birds and shorebirds may forage in flooded or fallow farm fields, while the Western Bluebird might find a useful post from which to catch insects. American Coots prefer wetlands with open water and emergent vegetation.

Whidbey Island

Ring-necked Pheasant, male — Skagit Valley

American Coot

Western Bluebird, male

Long-billed Curlews   Farm environment

Fences and posts make ideal perches for a number of birds that use meadows or their edges to hunt for food. Brewer's Blackbirds and European Starlings group together after the breeding season, forming large flocks in agricultural areas or wetlands.

Townsend's Solitaire

Western Meadowlark

European Starling

Brewer's Blackbird, male & female · Crockett Lake

California Quail chicks are precocial, meaning they are up and running right after hatching. Immediately pecking at the ground for food and following their parents, they keep close to the cover of underbrush.

An adult quail pair may join their brood with other quail families, then all adults will watch over the young together. One male typically acts as sentinel, perching on a higher point, ready to alert the group of potential danger, as the male shown here was doing.

California Quail chicks

California Quail, female with chicks

California Quail, female   Keystone Spit

California Quail, male   Crockett Lake

From summertime alpine breeding grounds to sea level beaches in winter and marsh or farmland during migration, the American Pipit makes use of diverse types of habitat throughout the year. Its tail bobbing behavior distinguishes it from similar looking "little brown birds."

Open areas, such as pastures or grassland, are appealing to Western Kingbirds.

Foulweather Bluff

Western Kingbird

Canada Geese   Ridgefield NWR

Snow Goose   Skagit Valley

Wilson's Snipe   Ridgefield NWR

A wetland is like an oasis in the long flight of a migratory bird. Stopovers in such places are essential for rest and refueling. Development of many of these areas makes preservation of our National Wildlife Refuges, such as Ridgefield, on the Columbia River near Vancouver, Washington, even more important.

Tundra Swans, juvenile & adult   Ridgefield NWR

Pied-billed Grebes and Ruddy Ducks may perform evasive underwater maneuvers to avoid detection, rather than fly away. Submerging most of its body, the Pied-billed Grebe leaves eyes and nostrils exposed. Ruddy Ducks will sink below the surface, then swim away underwater.

Ruddy Duck, male   Ridgefield NWR

Pied-billed Grebe   Deer Lagoon

A very secretive heron, the American Bittern blends well among reeds, moving very slowly with head pointed upward. If startled, it will freeze, then sway back and forth like grass in the wind.

American Bittern

American Bittern

Directly after catch

Capturing a snake of at least 30 inches with one quick strike looked easy for this Great Blue Heron, but ingesting it proved more challenging! It took the heron 15 minutes to get it contained.

Green Heron   Scriber Lake

Green Heron, juvenile

Green Heron, nestling

Black-crowned Night-Heron   Potholes Wildlife Area

Very intense about fishing, the Green Heron is one of the few bird species that will use tools, such as twigs, leaves, or even earthworms, to lure fish to the surface of the water for easier capture.

Belted Kingfisher, male Kennedys Lagoon

Belted Kingfisher, female

Snappy, rust colored, belly-bands make female Belted Kingfishers brighter than the males. Kingfishers are usually seen perched near a water source where they can quickly dive for fish. This one was on the floodgate between Crockett Lake and Puget Sound, on Whidbey Island.

Mallard, male   Floodgate at Crockett Lake

Floodgate at Crockett Lake

Virginia Rail   Edmonds Marsh

Red-winged Blackbird, female on nest
Nisqually NWR

Yellow-headed Blackbird, male   Othello

Yellow-headed Blackbird, female

Dense vegetation around wetland edges provides excellent cover for many bird species to safely forage and nest. A female Red-winged Blackbird is well concealed in her elevated nest among the cattail stalks (opposite page) and there are plenty of insects to feed hungry fledglings.

Secretive Virginia Rails readily navigate slippery reeds and mud with their long-toed feet.

Virginia Rail, juvenile

Red-winged Blackbird, fledgling

Red-winged Blackbird, male   Juanita Bay Park

65

Hooded Merganser, male

Bufflehead, male

Both diving ducks, Hooded Mergansers and Buffleheads nest in tree cavities. Hooded Mergansers rely heavily on cavities created by Pileated Woodpeckers while the smaller Buffleheads primarily use abandoned Northern Flicker nest holes.

Hooded Merganser, female with chicks   Earth Sanctuary

Wood Duck, female and chicks
Earth Sanctuary

Exotic-looking Wood Ducks may be found on ponds or wetlands near dense woods, where they prefer to nest in naturally occurring tree cavities. It is always a delight to see fluffy ducklings paddling around the pond with their mothers in the spring! Richly colored Cinnamon Teals also dabble in ponds but will hide their ground nest in surrounding vegetation.

Wood Duck, male

Cinnamon Teal, male _ Spencer Island

Waterfowl are often congregated with multiple species in close proximity before and after the breeding season.

Blue-winged Teal, male

Green-winged Teal, male

Greater White-fronted Goose
Union Bay Natural Area

Northern Pintail,
male & female
Anacortes

Redhead, female & male   Othello

American Wigeon, male & female

Gadwall, male & female

Recognizable by its elegantly shaded bill, the Ring-necked Duck's namesake (the dark neck ring), is difficult to see at a distance.

After slowly circling around while facing each other, two male Northern Shovelers erupted into an intense, splashing confrontation at Fir Island, Skagit Valley, in early March (top left). With enormous bills open, they flicked their wings out with force sending an upsurge of water.

Northern Shoveler, males in dispute

Lesser Scaup, male

Greater Scaup, female   Keystone Ferry Terminal

Ring-necked Duck, male   Whidbey Island

Multiple layers of foraging habitat in this wetland provide food for a variety of shorebirds, making it an ideal stopover on a long migration. Of course the exposed waders need to keep a watchful eye above for the fast flying Peregrine Falcon and Merlin that may try to make a meal out of them.

As unofficial sentinels, wary Black-bellied Plovers are quick to let out an alarm call. Give and take is the natural order here, as all creatures must eat.

Merlin

Peregrine Falcon

Whimbrel
Crockett Lake

Black-bellied Plover   Crockett Lake

Pectoral Sandpiper

American Avocet
Eastern WA

Shallow ponds and marsh wetlands attract long legged Black-necked Stilts and American Avocets, as well as Wilson's Phalaropes that breed in areas of Eastern Washington. All of these shorebirds are very graceful and elegant in appearance but won't hesitate to vehemently defend their nesting areas.

Wilson's Phalarope, male & female   Othello

Black-necked Stilts   Othello

American Avocet, non-breeding   Eastern WA

Black-necked Stilt   Othello

Wandering among the picklegrass near the edge of Crockett Lake, Greater and Lesser Yellowlegs look quite similar, except for the distinct difference in size.

Spotted Sandpipers are summertime breeders in much of Washington State, using a variety of fresh-water and estuarine habitats.

Spotted Sandpiper   Jimmy-Come-Lately Creek

Greater & Lesser Yellowlegs   Port Townsend

Long-billed Dowitcher   Crockett Lake

Short-billed Dowitcher, juvenile   Swan Lake

Western Sandpiper   Crockett Lake

With their different body, leg, and bill sizes, assorted species of shorebirds are able to use specific portions of shoreline exposed by changing tides or water levels without interfering with one another.

Using a quick up and down "stitching" motion, Long-billed Dowitchers probe the mud in shallow water for soft-bodied invertebrates.

Long-billed Dowitcher   Crockett Lake

Beach ~ Offshore

Where there is water, there will be birds. With a great deal of saltwater coastline and its more protected waterways along Puget Sound, Washington is a haven not only for resident bird populations but also migratory birds headed to and from the arctic and sub-arctic regions of the planet to breed. The bounty of the sea is brought up to the shore, where birds can access what they need.

Marbled Godwit, female   Ocean Shores

Dunlin

Damon Point State Park, Ocean Shores

Damon Point State Park hosts an array of migrating shorebirds every spring and fall.

Semipalmated Plover

Willet   Tokeland

Long-billed Curlew, female & American Crow   Damon Point State Park

75

Flying over the ocean beaches in straight lines, Brown Pelicans are more frequently seen in Washington than they were previously. After breeding in California and Mexico, they fly northward along the coast in post-breeding dispersal and are now abundant as far north as Grays Harbor in the summer months.

Murres and murrelets might be seen offshore or while riding a ferry on Puget Sound.

Marbled Murrelet   Mukilteo

Common Murre   Keystone Spit

Related to puffins, Rhinoceros Auklets have impressive breeding plumage. Highly skilled at fishing, these dedicated parents will hold several fish in their bills for hours, waiting until after dusk to fly ashore with this meal for their single chick, tucked safely away in a burrow.

Rhinoceros Auklet, non-breeding

Rhinoceros Auklet, with fish

Rhinoceros Auklet, diving

Rhinoceros Auklet   Keystone Spit

Red-necked Phalarope, juvenile   Keystone Spit

These birds may come closer to land when foraging for crustaceans or shallow-dwelling invertebrates. Keeping waterways clean and healthy, free of polluted run-off and litter, will help ensure the abundance of sea life available for seabirds and humans.

Common Loon with crab   Ocean Shores area

Surf Scoter, male   Penn Cove

Common Loon, non-breeding   Deception Pass State Park

Brant   Edmonds

Whidbey Island, near Keystone Spit

Loons typically are seen further out, so it was a welcome surprise to find this Pacific Loon close to shore at Whidbey Island's Keystone Spit. A thin "chin-strap" distinguishes this loon from the similar looking Common Loon in non-breeding plumage.

Groups of Brant may be seen riding waves at the edge of the surf in certain areas of Puget Sound during winter.

Pacific Loon, non-breeding   Keystone Spit

Pelagic Cormorant with nesting material

Sea cave nest sites

Pelagic Cormorants look very elegant in their iridescent breeding plumage. We watched several in late May at Cape Flattery on the Olympic Peninsula's northwest tip, as they flew into the nearby sea caves with grasses or seaweed collected for nesting material. Using their own guano, they adhere the nest to a narrow, high cliff ledge.

Tatoosh Island, Cape Flattery, Washington

Double-crested Cormorants   Crockett Lake

Out of the water with wings spread and tail fanned, this is a familiar posture for Double-crested Cormorants. Absorbent feathers reduce buoyancy, allowing for deeper dives, but then must be dried out to prevent the birds from getting too cold.

Brandt's Cormorant

Double-crested Cormorant
Crockett Lake area

Osprey with sole catch   Bush Point

Osprey with
salmonid catch

Osprey with
Starry Flounder catch

Ospreys return each spring to breed, nesting along the coast, Puget Sound, and inland waters where fishing is plentiful. The original "Seahawk," an Osprey was the inspiration for the Seattle football team name.

Osprey pair and nest

Osprey   Bush Point

Horned Grebe, non-breeding

Horned Grebe   Ebey's Landing

Eared Grebe   Eastern WA

Grebes, like loons, have feet positioned far back on their bodies, allowing for maximum propulsion under water but making them quite awkward on land.

Western Grebe

Western Grebe

Red-necked Grebe   Edmonds

Jetty Island, a man made landmass about five miles long, just offshore from Everett, is an area where Caspian Terns have been known to breed. A rare commodity near a highly industrialized waterfront, shorebirds and gulls also use this precious, undeveloped habitat close to an urban setting.

Caspian Terns   Ocean Shores

Mew Gull   Padilla Bay

Caspian Tern, adult with juvenile Jetty Island

Glaucous-winged Gull

Mew Gull with crustacean

Western Gull   Ocean Shores

A variety of gulls commonly occur along the Washington coast and shores of Puget Sound, where they feast on a smorgasbord of seafood. Some are migratory species, just passing through or possibly staying for the winter, such as Bonaparte's and California Gulls.

Readily distinguishable with their red bills, dark back and wings, and black feet, Heermann's Gulls breed south of the United States and come north in July to spend the non-breeding season here, heading back south mid-October.

Bonaparte's Gull with prey, non-breeding

Bonaparte's Gull, breeding

California Gull

Heermann's Gull   Keystone Spit

Attractive Red-breasted Mergansers breed farther north and winter farther south than the other American mergansers. Preferring a saltwater environment, they can often be seen off Whidbey Island's Keystone Spit and other areas of Puget Sound during the winter, catching fish in their serrated bills.

Differently shaped white facial patches distinguish similar looking male Barrow's and Common Goldeneyes. Both species are divers, with Common Goldeneyes found throughout Washington in the winter. Strong site fidelity brings Barrow's Goldeneyes back to certain areas such as Penn Cove, off Whidbey Island, each winter.

Barrow's Goldeneye, male

Common Goldeneye, male

Red-breasted Merganser, male   Bush Point

Common Goldeneye, female

86   Red-breasted Merganser, female   Keystone Spit

Handsome Harlequin Ducks are sure to turn heads when they form large wintering rafts.

Penn Cove, Whidbey Island

Harlequin Duck, male   Coupeville

An icon of the Northwest, the Great Blue Heron can be found in many habitats, from shoreline or lagoon to open fields. Diverse eating habits that may include fish, invertebrates, amphibians, reptiles and birds contribute to this array of suitable living arrangements.

Extensive heron nesting rookeries are quite a sight, yet some individuals have successfully taken to nesting on dolphins at the Coupeville / Keystone Ferry terminal.

Great Blue Heron, juvenile, Crockett Lake

Great Blue Heron, nestling   Keystone Ferry Terminal

Pigeon Guillemots are being studied on Whidbey Island in an ongoing citizen-science research project. Participating for several years, we monitored the number of nest burrows used at one high-bluff colony site. Photographs Craig took helped to identify what fish the adult birds were carrying to the young.

Pigeon Guillemots   Keystone Spit

Pigeon Guillemot nestlings in burrow

Pigeon Guillemot with Cod

Pigeon Guillemot delivering (Gunnel) fish to burrow   Bush Point

Our most common wintering shorebird, Dunlin have a long, downward drooping, black bill. Sanderlings, also familiar winter residents, may be seen pecking and probing at the wave line.

The smallest of our local "peeps," Least Sandpipers might be found on the shore or, more often, in a saltwater marsh habitat. Though uncommon in this area, Whimbrels are comfortable in a variety of salt or fresh-water coastal habitats.

Sanderling

Least Sandpiper

Whimbrel

Several shorebird species depend on rocky shores to make a living. Non-migratory Black Oystercatchers forage, roost and nest on the rocks. Ruddy and Black Turnstones are named for their behavior of turning over pebbles and other small objects to find invertebrates.

Killdeer are a common plover that may be found year-round, either on the beach or far from water. With big eyes positioned on the sides of their heads, they see almost all the way around them.

Black Turnstone

Ruddy Turnstone

Black Oystercatcher   Keystone Spit

Killdeer   Mutiny Bay

Killdeer   Keystone Spit

Great Horned Owl

Brown Creeper

Steller's Jay, juvenile

Foothills ~ Mountain

Washington's foothills and mountain ranges host a variety of species hardy enough to withstand the extreme weather. Some birds migrate to higher elevations only for summer months to take advantage of abundant insects and wildflowers when raising their young.

Forests of the foothills and mountains provide habitat for some species that also occur in the lowlands.

Mountain Chickadee

Black-capped Chickadee

Mountain Chickadees live in montane coniferous forests year-round. When weather is particularly harsh in the winter, they may move downslope to find food. Similar looking Black-capped Chickadees have buff colored sides and lack the white "eyebrow."

Mountain Chickadee   Wenas Basin

One would be hard pressed to spot this female Sooty Grouse against the chipped rock. Cryptic plumage provides her perfect camouflage.

Sooty Grouse, female foraging

Sooty Grouse, male performing mating call   Hurricane Ridge

In addition to the many bird species found among Puget Sound's diverse habitats, still others are attracted to our ocean beaches, alpine meadows and desert areas east of the Cascades. Having such differing habitats within a few hours' drive truly adds to the wealth of our region's avian treasures.

Clark's Nutcracker   Wenas Basin

Gray Jay   Hurricane Ridge

Gray Jay   Hurricane Ridge

Mountain Bluebird, male   Wenas Basin

Index

A

Auklet, Rhinoceros, 77
Avocet, American, 71

B

Bittern, American, 60
Blackbird
  Brewer's, 55
  Red-winged, 64, 65
  Yellow-headed, 65
Bluebird
  Mountain, 95
  Western, 54
Brant, 79
Bufflehead, 66
Bushtit, 14

C

Chickadee
  Black-capped, 11, 93
  Chestnut-backed, 19
  Mountain, 93
Coot, American, 54
Cormorant
  Brandt's, 81
  Double-crested, 81
  Pelagic, 80
Cowbird, Brown-headed, 6
Creeper, Brown, 23, 92
Crossbill, Red, 18
Crow, American, 41, 75
Curlew, Long-billed, 54, 75

D

Dove
  Mourning, 34
Dowitcher
  Long-billed, 73
  Short-billed, 73
Duck
  Harlequin, 87
  Ring-necked, 69
  Ruddy, 59
  Wood, 67
Dunlin, 75, 90

E

Eagle, Bald, 51
Egret, Great, 58

F

Falcon, Peregrine, 49, 50, 70
Finch
  Cassin's, 4
  House, 26
  Purple, 26
Flicker, Northern, 30
Flycatcher
  Ash-throated, 38
  Olive-sided, 38
  Pacific-slope, 22
  Willow, 38

G

Gadwall, 68
Godwit, Marbled, 74
Goldeneye
  Common, 86
  Barrow's, 86
Goldfinch
  American, 27
  Lesser, 27
Goose
  Canada, 58
  Greater White-fronted, 68
  Snow, 58
Grebe
  Eared, 83
  Horned, 83
  Pied-billed, 59
  Red-necked, 83
  Western, 83
Grosbeak
  Black-headed, 9
  Evening, 9
Grouse, Sooty, 94
Guillemot, Pigeon, 89
Gull
  Bonaparte's, 85
  California, 85
  Glaucous-winged, 84
  Heermann's, 85
  Mew, 84
  Western, 85
Gyrfalcon, 49

H

Harrier, Northern, 44
Hawk
  Cooper's, 35
  Red-tailed, 46, 47
  Rough-legged, 48
  Sharp-shinned, 35
  Swainson's, 49
Heron
  Great Blue, 61, 88
  Green, 62
Hummingbird
  Anna's, 13
  Rufous, 12

J

Jay
  Gray, 95
  Steller's, 32, 92
Junco, Dark-eyed, 17

K

Kestrel, American, 50
Killdeer, 91
Kingbird
  Eastern, 22
  Western, 57
Kingfisher, Belted, 63
Kinglet
  Golden-crowned, 10
  Ruby-crowned, 11

L

Loon
  Common, 78
  Pacific, 79

M

Magpie, Black-billed, 32
Mallard, 63
Martin, Purple, 53
Meadowlark, Western, 55
Merganser
  Hooded, 66
  Red-breasted, 86
Merlin, 49, 70

Murre, Common, 76
Murrelet, Marbled, 76

N

Night-Heron, Black-crowned, 62
Nutcracker, Clark's, 95
Nuthatch
  Red-breasted, 33
  White-breasted, 38

O

Oriole, Bullock's, 8
Osprey, 82
Owl
  Barn, 37
  Barred, 37
  Great Horned, 36, 92
  Short-eared, 45
  Snowy, 45
Oystercatcher, Black, 91

P

Pelican, Brown, 76
Phalarope
  Red-necked, 78
  Wilson's, 71
Pheasant, Ring-necked, 54
Phoebe, Say's, 39
Pigeon
  Band-tailed, 34
  Rock, 34
Pintail, Northern, 68
Pipit, American, 57
Plover
  Black-bellied, 70
  Semipalmated, 75

Q

Quail, California, 56

R

Rail, Virginia, 64, 65
Raven, Common, 40
Redhead, 68
Robin, American, 21

S

Sanderling, 90
Sandpiper
  Least, 90
  Pectoral, 70
  Spotted, 72
  Western, 73
Sapsucker, Red-breasted, 28, 92
Scaup
  Greater, 69
  Lesser, 69
Scoter, Surf, 78
Scrub-Jay, Western, 32
Shoveler, Northern, 69
Shrike
  Loggerhead, 42
  Northern, 42
Siskin, Pine, 18
Snipe, Wilson's, 58
Solitaire, Townsend's, 38, 55
Sparrow
  Chipping, 39
  Fox, 25
  Golden-crowned, 24
  House, 25
  Lark, 42
  Lincoln's, 22
  Savannah, 42
  Song, 25
  White-crowned, 24
Starling, European, 55
Stilt, Black-necked, 71
Swallow
  Barn, 53
  Cliff, 52
  Northern Rough-winged, 53
  Tree, 52
  Violet-green, 52
Swan, Tundra, 58

T

Tanager, Western, 8
Teal
  Cinnamon, 67
  Blue-winged, 68
  Green-winged, 68

Tern, Caspian, 84
Thrasher, Sage, 39
Thrush
  Hermit, 21
  Swainson's, 23, 39
  Varied, 20
Towhee, Spotted, 16
Turnstone
  Black, 91
  Ruddy, 91

V

Vireo, Warbling, 4
Vulture, Turkey, 49

W

Warbler
  Audubon's, 6
  Myrtle, 6
  Orange-crowned, 5
  Townsend's, 6
  Wilson's, 5
  Yellow, 4
  Yellow-rumped, 6
Waxwing, Cedar, 7
Whimbrel, 70, 90
Wigeon, American, 68
Willet, 75
Woodpecker
  Downy, 29
  Hairy, 29
  Lewis's, 28
  Pileated, 31
Wood-Pewee, Western, 22
Wren
  Bewick's, 15
  House, 15
  Marsh, 43
  Pacific (Winter), 15

Y

Yellowlegs
  Greater, 72
  Lesser, 72
Yellowthroat, Common, 5

Acknowledgments

Dr. Dennis Paulson, prolific author and educator on subjects such as birds and dragonflies (*Dragonflies and Damselflies of the West,* winner of a 2009 National Outdoor Book Award).
Dan Pedersen, author of *Whidbey Island's Special Places,* www.whidbeywriter.com.   **Lynda Blakely**, retired educator and avid birdwatcher.   **Renee Matson**, educator and bird enthusiast.

References: The Birds Of North America Online, Cornell Lab of Ornithology, www.bna.birds.cornell.edu   Seattle Audubon Society, www.seattleaudubon.org
Pigeon Guillemot Survey, www.whidbeyaudubon.org   Bell, Brian H., Gregory Kennedy. 2006. Birds of Washington State. Lone Pine Publishing International, Inc. Auburn, WA.